A Riddle Flap Book
WHO AM I?

By Betty Birney / Illustrated by Lisa Berrett

I am tiny and gray.
I have dainty pink feet.
There is no piece of cheese
That I won't try to eat.

I am giant and gray.
I weigh more than a ton.
I think picking up peanuts
Can be lots of fun.

I'm the King of the Beasts.
I have a load ROAR!
I sleep most of the day
And I purr when I snore.

My feathers are bright.
I repeat what you say.
If you give me a cracker
I'll whistle, "Hooray!"

My head is high up.
My long neck is slender.
I nibble the treetops
Where leaves are most tender.

You'll find me on ice.
I am all white and black.
I love to go swimming
To hunt for a snack.